Earth Keepers

Earth Keepers

Text by JOAN ANDERSON   Photographs by GEORGE ANCONA

A GULLIVER GREEN BOOK   HARCOURT BRACE & COMPANY   San Diego   New York   London

Requests for permission to make copies of any part of the work should be
mailed to: Permissions Department, Harcourt Brace & Company,
8th Floor, Orlando, Florida 32887.

Excerpt from "Think Little" in *A Continuous Harmony: Essays Cultural and
Agricultural*, copyright © 1972 by Wendell Berry, reprinted by permission of
Harcourt Brace & Company. Excerpt from *Ox Against the Storm: A Biography of
Tanaka Shozo, Japan's Conservationist Pioneer* by Kenneth Strong (Vancouver:
UBC Press 1977) is reprinted with permission. Copyright University of British
Columbia Press. All rights reserved.

The photograph on page 27 first appeared in *Riverkeeper*,
by George Ancona. Copyright © 1990 by George Ancona.
Reproduced with the permission of Macmillan Publishing Company.

The photographs in this book were printed by Gene Merinov,
Aurora Color Labs, New York City.

Library of Congress Cataloging-in-Publication Data
Anderson, Joan.
Earth keepers/text by Joan Anderson; photographs by George Ancona. —1st ed.
p. cm.
"Gulliver books."
Summary: Discusses the work of three environmental protection
groups who are striving to help save the Earth from destruction.
ISBN 0-15-242199-8
1. Environmental protection—United States—Citizen
participation—Case studies—Juvenile literature. 2. Human ecology—Juvenile
literature. [1. Environmental protection.] I. Ancona, George, ill. II. Title.
TD171.7.A54 1993 363.7′00525—dc20 92-38627

Book design by Camilla Filancia
First edition A B C D E
Printed in Singapore

To Andrew and Shelly Jones-Wilkins,
for making me conscious of the pure joy that comes
from living close to the land   —J. A.

To John Cronin, the Riverkeeper   —G. A.

Many thanks to everyone who enlightened us about the
care and feeding of the earth. We are grateful to the crew of
the sloop *Clearwater*, who welcomed us aboard, and espe-
cially to Nancy Bernstein. Jane Wiseman of Greenthumb
opened the gates of gardens and gardeners all over New
York and arranged for us to get closer to the land in the
city. Thank you, Jane and Malinda Futrell. Blue Magruder
of Earthwatch introduced us to Lynn Rogers and the Forest
Service people in Minnesota. We gained insight from Wally
Elton of the Student Conservation Association and Angela
Cook, Forest Ranger in Ely, Minnesota.

Introduction

How many of us today truly feel part of the land on which we live? How connected are we to nature, to trees and plants, rivers and streams, dark rich soil, and to all creatures big and small?

In these times, when many of us live in crowded cities or bustling suburbs, it is easy to feel isolated from the land. Our lives have become so mechanized we rarely think about how the world works. We have trouble seeing the earth beneath our feet or the trees above our heads when we are surrounded by concrete, steel, and asphalt. While it's simple to turn on a faucet, how many of us know where our water really comes from? Or where the trash goes after the garbageman picks it up? When we lose our connection with the natural world, we do not understand how an animal's extinction or the destruction of a forest affects us.

Nevertheless, the warnings are real. We can no longer feast on the resources of this planet without taking care of them, too. Each and every one of us must reach out and make friends with nature. But how?

First we need to understand the importance of the natural things in our lives. Through the ages, such cultures as the Yanomama of the Amazon, the Aborigines of Australia, and the Native Americans of this country have understood people's relationship with the environment, have developed a kinship with nature. They see themselves as part of the web of life, referring to the earth as mother and to animals as sisters and brothers. It makes sense, doesn't it, that if we look at nature as family, we will care for it as we do our own human families.

In this book you will meet people who have dedicated their lives to reestablishing their connection to nature, and learn how they are encouraging others to do the same. Nancy Bernstein, an environmental educator aboard the teaching schooner *Clearwater*, works to get people to befriend the Hudson River; Malinda Futrell is creating urban farms where for a long time there was only cement; wildlife biologist Lynn Rogers has made friends with black bears and other animals to ensure that the Forest Service manages their habitat responsibly. These people by no means represent the total picture of worthy earth keepers, but their work and their programs stand as an example of how each of us can connect with nature.

"I could swear that the river has its own soul that jumps right out and dances along. Each little fish spawning, each tidal cycle, each person intimately connected with it are all part of that identity. There really is a lot to rejoice over."

— NANCY BERNSTEIN

All is quiet on the sleepy Hudson River except for the occasional splash of jumping fish or the honk of geese flying in formation overhead. The blanket of mist that has cloaked the river throughout the night has evaporated, revealing a sturdy dock and a large sailboat secured to it. For the past twenty-two years, this majestic sloop and the people who sail her have been dedicated to making people aware of the river's importance in their lives and getting help to clean it up.

It is 6:45 A.M., time for the crew of the sloop *Clearwater* to rise and shine. Environmental educator Nancy Bernstein emerges from the cramped sleeping quarters beneath the deck of the 106-foot sailing vessel.

"I could swear that the river has its own soul that jumps right out and dances along," she says, eager to spend another day sharing her river experiences with the hundred or so visitors who come aboard. "The wonderful things of this earth are being challenged, and I feel a need to take part in keeping them alive."

Soon she is joined by the rest of the crew, who share similar dreams. When folksinger Pete Seeger started the Clearwater organization, the Hudson River was thoroughly polluted. By bringing people to the river and talking about its importance, many of them have become activists who now care for the river. The Clearwater people feel that environmental awareness is a matter of helping people understand how the earth works.

"The sloop's greatest success has been to focus attention on the river," says Nancy. "*Clearwater* has proved that the dream of a cleaner river can come true."

In the galley below, freshly brewed coffee perks away on the wood-burning stove. The cook sounds the breakfast gong and eight men and five women gather around the table. They eagerly dig in to melon, yogurt, orange juice, and Cream of Wheat topped with maple syrup. Missing is the bacon, sausage, and junk food encased in hard-to-dispose-of packaging.

"The people on the boat are vegetarians," Nancy explains. "We are trying to live our lives in ways that will be kind to the environment, and that means honoring all living things, including animals."

Nearby stands a compost bucket the crew use to recycle their refuse in. When vegetable peels and food scraps decompose they make a rich, active material that improves soil quality. "Most stuff doesn't have to become garbage," says first mate Josh Gordon. "If you recycle, it can be used in another way."

Up on deck a bucket brigade removes human waste from the sloop's outhouse. When the *Clearwater* was first built, a chemical toilet was installed. After a time the crew felt compromised. They were working to stop the dumping of raw sewage in the river and yet doing it themselves. So

the chemical toilet was removed and an outhouse set up. The crew take the contents to a landfill area when they are in port.

"All hands on deck!" shouts Captain Beth Doxsee, who has had her hand on *Clearwater*'s tiller for eight years. Today the crew are preparing a sail for fourth and fifth graders.

"They're some of my favorite passengers," Nancy says. "Kids have a strong sense of what's right and wrong, and they tend to see the issues pretty clearly.

"Anyone want to go sailing?" Nancy shouts to the children approaching the gangway. "Yeah!" a resounding chorus echoes back. "Well then, come aboard!

"We want people to make a connection to nature," Nancy explains. "We figure a good way to do that with the river is to get kids to make friends with it. That way they might take a greater interest in caring for it."

"Hands-on education is what we're about," says the sloop's engineer. "When kids get excited about catching a fish or raising a sail, I feel hopeful. They are going to be the ones making policy in the future.

"Ready on the throat," he yells to the kids who have lined up on either side of the deck to raise the 1½-ton sail. "Ready on the peak. All right then, hand over hand, pull!" Grunts and heavy breathing can be heard. Gradually the massive canvas flapping overhead drowns out all other sounds, and once again the wind pulls the *Clearwater* out of the channel and into the river. Soon the shore, with its glistening marsh grasses, fades in the distance.

As the wooden hull plows through the water a spell of enchantment falls over these first-time sailors. Suddenly the vessel heels to port and a spray of cool water blows across the deck, delighting everyone.

"Y'know, a few years ago," Nancy tells the children surrounding her, "the river was so polluted with sewage and toxic waste that if you fell overboard you had to be taken to the hospital for shots."

Because of Clearwater's program, ordinary citizens learned they could make a difference and improve their environment. Today people can swim and boat in the Hudson River. And six communities use river water for their household needs.

"We've gotten people like your parents to write their legislators and change the laws," Josh tells the kids, "and it's made a difference. Back in nineteen eighty-four, there were only eight toxins banned from the river. Now we have added two hundred more to the list!"

Clearwater also has an environmental action department that actively lobbies in Washington and Albany. They helped pass the Clean Water Act, which makes pollution a crime.

Looking at algae

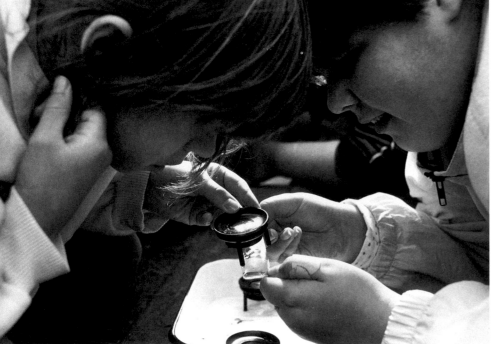

"Want to see how clean the water really is?" Nancy and a bunch of kids head for midship, where a chemistry station has been set up.

"Just because water is clear," she says, holding up several vials of river water, "doesn't mean it's clean. You can't always see pollution."

She performs a test that shows how much oxygen is in the water. "Years ago people got rid of all their waste by dumping it in the river. New York City alone was dumping two hundred and twenty million gallons of sewage into the river daily. Most of us still don't think about where toilet water goes, right? But think about it: sewage from your house goes down a drain, then into the river. That's when the trouble begins. As more and more waste is dumped into the river it creates bacteria, which multiply, robbing water of oxygen."

"So what?" one of the kids pipes up.

The children learn that fish need to live in water that has an oxygen content of five parts per million. Just like people, who couldn't walk around on Earth without oxygen in the air to breathe, fish need oxygen, too. If a river is depleted of oxygen, eventually it will become a dead river.

"Who wants to live beside a dead anything?" Nancy asks. "Before we began cleaning up the river, the fish and plant life were dying."

Connecting with the river doesn't take long on these three-hour sails. Every minute is spent talking about, relating to, and touching the river.

Members of the crew have thrown a trawl net overboard. Soon they are ready for the kids to help haul it aboard. As the net is pulled out of the water a wide variety of wiggly fish come with it. The fish are quickly placed in a tank.

"We're happy that the fish are back and we're able to at least eat the shad," Nancy says. "Too bad we can't eat the others. If we did we'd be eating PCBs—polychlorinated biphenyls—and PCBs can make you sick. Not the kind of sick that'll give you just a fever or a runny nose, but a long-term sickness, like cancer."

"Ugh," one kid exclaims. A freckle-faced boy asks how the PCBs got in the fish.

"A major American company dumped PCBs in the river back in nineteen seventy-seven, and this chemical got into the food chain. What happens is that the big fish eat the smaller fish, which have eaten plankton contaminated with PCBs. Soon the larger fish are also contaminated, which makes them unhealthy to eat.

"The fish were here first," Nancy continues. "Do you think this is how we should treat our river, its fish, or ourselves?"

"No way!" the kids shout back.

Although the Clearwater message is serious, nothing can take away the joy and magic felt aboard the sailing ship.

"The good news is that by changing the laws about sewage being dumped in the river, the Hudson now has a healthy oxygen level, which allows the fish to live." Nancy grabs a banjo and urges the kids to settle in and enjoy the environment that surrounds them.

With the wind blowing in their faces and the rhythmical sound of water lapping against the side of the boat, the crew begin singing a few old sea chanties. Then they add some songs about water and waste. If nothing else, the fourth and fifth graders who set sail this morning will leave the *Clearwater* singing of the need for just that . . . clear water.

"Animals need water, people
need it, too.
Keep it clean for me, and I'll
keep it clean for you.
Really clean water is getting
mighty rare,
so if we want to save it,
people have to care . . ."

Sharing the fun of steering the tiller

Clearwater is caring for a big river and the crew know they can't do it alone. "Cleaning up the river takes many hands," Nancy claims. "The more people involved the better. My role is to educate and inform, and I hope that others take it on themselves to vote for laws that protect our waters."

"It's gratifying when we run into a mother or a father bringing their kids for a sail, just as they were brought fifteen or twenty years ago. The awareness is catching," says Josh Gordon. As he speaks, a motorboat passes, and the skipper toots his horn. "That's the river keeper. He's one of the people who police the river."

John Cronin, the river keeper, is an ex-commercial fisherman who decided to go after people and companies who are polluting the river. He not only takes people to court to make them stop what they are doing but he is also responsible for the writing of new laws to protect the river. He is another example of a citizen who decided to make a difference.

Clearwater also offers a land-based program, which is conducted along the banks of the Hudson River. Environmentalist Ken Yaso gathers youngsters together and drops a series of maps across the lawn so they can visualize the length and breadth of the river. "This three hundred and twenty-five mile river is one source of water that flows to and from the ocean," he explains, pointing to New York City and beyond. "Kind of impressive looking, isn't it? This river is an arm of the sea, and it affects animal and plant life all the way up to Nova Scotia. With tides coming in twice a day, all sorts of garbage that pollutes the river washes up on our shores."

Part of the day's program includes a beach cleanup. Outfitting the kids with work gloves and clipboards to record their finds, he leads them along the shore. "We're going to clean up this beach," he says. "You'll become detectives in the process, finding all sorts of things that could have been dumped overboard by a foreign freighter or a cargo ship."

Before the day is over, students onshore, just like the passengers aboard *Clearwater*, come to understand that the river is home to many living things. Ken and his partner drag a seine net in the water and soon haul in a huge variety of species: hogchokers, shiners, pumpkinseed sunfish, and even a couple of largemouth bass. By getting their feet wet, digging for crabs in the mud flats, picking up litter, and soaking up the tranquil pleasures of just being beside the river, these kids are eager to go home and make a difference. Some will adopt a stream, making regular visits to clean up the trash; others will collect water from pipes that run into the river and take it to be tested; still others will organize week-long beach cleanups. Some classes will write to their legislators for better environmental laws. Together they have learned one lesson: each of us can pitch in and help.

"It's vital that we work to be part of the solution by being responsible for our actions," Nancy says.

Today's passengers disembark from the *Clearwater* and take home a true river experience as well as a changed life view. Now it's up to them to make a difference. "Once we make the connection between the river, ourselves, and the need to take action, there's hope," says Nancy Bernstein. "We will reverse pollution."

The people of the schooner *Clearwater* will continue to teach others that there isn't a mythical place called "away" where we can throw our trash and deposit our refuse and have it become someone else's problem. The truth is that pollution is everyone's problem.

"The care of rivers is not a question of rivers, but of the human heart."
—TANAKA SHOZO

"God didn't create this earth to look like a huge sore. I'm trying to do what I can to make it beautiful."
                                          —MALINDA FUTRELL

The late summer air is heavy with exhaust fumes, cement dust, and general urban pollution. An occasional beam of sunlight squeezes between the apartment buildings, allowing a tinge of color and light into an otherwise dull city block. Somehow amongst the hard edges and layers of mortar a field of green has managed to flower out of the rubble. As the morning glories signal a new day, the gate of the Sixth Street and Avenue B Garden is opened.

"Welcome to our garden," Malinda Futrell says warmly to passersby, who look with genuine curiosity at the sight of such lush, unexpected greenery.

Her friend and cofounder Nancy Paye unlocks the chain-link gate and opens it as wide as it will go. "This is city-owned land. We just manage it for the city. Good use of the land, don't you think?"

Every inch of space in this corner lot is used to cultivate the soil. Here, 105 "urban farmers" each pay twelve dollars a year to lease their tiny four-by-eight-foot plots.

"They can do anything they want with their land," Malinda says, her eyes sparkling as she surveys the diversity. "Each plot is a little thumbprint." Typical vegetable and flower plots are interspersed with meadows and wildflowers, peaceful corners bulging with fragrant herbs, and even a grape arbor. "There are many important things going on here. We've regenerated the soil and that's good. After all, God created healthy soil. It's up to us to take care of it. And the other thing is that all the people in the neighborhood are connecting to nature."

"Just nine years ago this corner was the neighborhood garbage dump as well as home to drug dealers and addicts," Malinda says.

"Most of us hated the place," Joanee Freedom, another garden cofounder, chimes in. "But one day I noticed a tomato plant growing right up out of all the trash. I couldn't believe my eyes! I immediately gathered up stones and bricks to make a little protective wall around the plant."

Soon thereafter a man named Charlie Paye cleared a small plot and planted a garden. It was his little creation that got Malinda thinking. A native of rural North Carolina, Malinda had come to the city in search of a better life, only to find herself longing for the land she'd left behind. "What was I doing here with all this noise and cement and no soil to dig my hands in?"

If he can do it, I sure can, Malinda thought, and within a matter of days she sought permission from the block association to start digging.

On July 19, 1983, "with beauty on my mind and love in my heart," a very determined Malinda began the backbreaking job of hauling away the rubble. For one whole year, she and two others labored. Gradually more neighbors pitched in, and the more space they cleared, the more they wanted to clear.

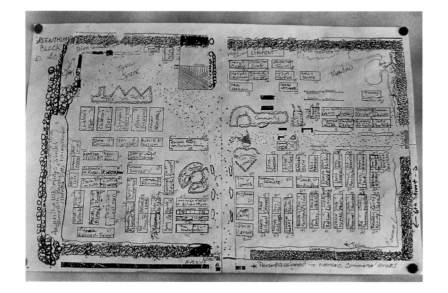

When the residents had the entire lot cleared, they sought help from a city gardening program called Operation Greenthumb, which leases more than 1,000 city-owned lots to 550 city gardens. "The only stipulation Greenthumb has," Malinda says, "is that we welcome the public inside several times a week. I try to have the gate open as much as we can. You know, beauty has a way of making people feel better."

Greenthumb encourages beautification, and it also encourages people to make vacant lots fruitful. Most of the city's gardens supply enough fresh produce that the gardeners, and many of their lucky friends, no longer need to purchase vegetables at the grocery store.

It was pretty obvious to the Greenthumb people that they had a woman of great will and determination in Malinda. They were quick to supply the initial topsoil, fencing, lumber, and assorted garden tools to get Malinda's garden going. Greenthumb even helped Malinda and her friends design their lot so they would have individual plots as well as common space.

Now, nine summers later, a full-fledged urban farm flourishes.

On this early September morning it is the turn of Malinda and fellow gardener Cheryl to act as water brigade. It's not a simple chore. There are no readily accessible spigots to connect the hose to. They have to drag hundreds of feet of hose out onto the city street and connect it to the corner hydrant. As the water begins gushing through, they fill up a dozen or so giant barrels from which the various plot owners fill up their watering cans.

A group of preschoolers from P.S. 122 frolics into the garden. "Hey, garden mother," they shout to Malinda, "how are you today?" But they are too excited to wait for an answer and they run to their own plot.

"Look at these carrots," an excited little girl says, yanking a bunch out of the moist soil for everyone to see. Nearby a classmate is scavenging the string bean vines, collecting every last one.

Avenue B Garden has several school plots. "These kids don't get a chance to see where vegetables come from," says their teacher, Cheryl Marie Taylor. "Here they learn how things grow. We come once a week, first to plant, then to water and weed. Now, in the fall, harvest is the real fun part."

Life inside the fence is calm and peaceful. As the day goes on single men, mothers with children, older people, and families come and go. Some call the garden a refuge. Others refer to it as an oasis. It is definitely a place to feel safe from the turbulence of the city streets.

"After I'm in here for just a few minutes, I fail to hear the racket outside," one gardener says.

"It's my backyard," says another. "Sure beats sitting on my apartment steps."

Each farmer cares for his or her individual plot and part of the common space that needs tending. "Everyone is responsible for a section of the border," Malinda says. She walks along the carefully laid brick path, yanking out blades of grass that are peeking through the cracks. The border, with its eight-year growth of hemlocks and evergreens, hollyhocks and bushes, is responsible for the intimacy one feels in this magic place. "The border shuts out the world around us and allows us some peace."

Two mothers sit chatting under the shade of a weeping willow, while a single woman meditates in the corner of the communal herb garden. A family enjoys their breakfast in a patio space, while an earnest man is laying tile under a nearby grape arbor.

"God created his earth to look beautiful," Malinda says. "I think we're helping the cause."

Reclaiming the soil is the biggest challenge in the adverse conditions offered to city farmers. Each plot sits aboveground. The gardeners dig down two feet and replace the beaten earth with layers of fresh soil and compost. Additional soil, trucked in by Operation Greenthumb, tops off each plot.

"When I put my hands in dirt," Malinda says, "I feel love. This is what we come from, you know. This is what we go back to.

"We don't add chemical fertilizer," she says, quick to point it out. "It isn't good for the earth, and besides, many people are allergic to it. We've found the stuff to be so strong that you can't plant for two or three weeks because it will burn the seeds and kill nearby healthy roots."

Instead of chemicals, the gardeners use cow and horse manure and peat moss. "Most soil is fixable," Malinda confidently states. "You just have to work with it."

COMMUNITY COMPOST

CONTRIBUTIONS WELCOME

GROUP:

ACCEPTABLE   PLEASE DON'T BRING

Nearby sits a huge compost bin in which the gardeners place their vegetable and fruit peelings as well as fallen leaves, weeds, and grass clippings. Organic waste such as this constitutes a quarter of New York City's trash, and Avenue B Garden is doing its part to recycle.

By using compost, the gardeners are returning their organic matter to the soil, which in turn improves plant growth. "Everyone's a winner in the recycling process," Malinda points out.

Outside the garden are rows of bins for the neighborhood to dispose of their cans, bottles, and plastics. "We're trying to get the people beyond our garden to care," Malinda explains.

There seem to be as many different reasons for gardening as there are gardeners.

The Eros family waited a year for their plot. "This garden is the only way to survive New York City in the summer," Jeannie Eros says as she ties her morning glories to a newly erected trellis. "It's the biggest and safest yard we have to hang out in."

Clear across the garden a young man builds a Japanese-style garden where he hopes to come and meditate. "Because the city is so aggressive, I come here to calm down and find some peace," he says.

Nearby, a woman named Connie has stopped on her way to work to look at her wild meadow. "I've let all my various flowers and grasses grow from seed. It's a little bit of country on the Lower East Side," she says, delighted with her spot.

Nancy Paye and her husband, Charlie, eat out of their garden all year long. "It's multipurpose," Nancy says. "We get lots of gifts out of it, and we share the food with our neighbors . . . and the smells we get!" She squeezes a basil leaf between her fingers. "Fresh food! Nothing like it."

Just one plot over from the Payes' stands perhaps the most unique use of a four-by-eight-foot plot. A sculptor named Ed has constructed a work of art that stands approximately three stories high. "I got sick of all the broken toys and discarded treasures people put out for the garbagemen to pick up. To me, these things are beautiful. So little by little I began to cart the stuff off, and inspiration led me to build this sculpture." Ed climbs up the side of his piece of art, eventually perching himself on a platform. "This is one way of cleaning up the neighborhood, right?"

All over the city, community gardens are revitalizing the soil and uplifting human spirits. With Greenthumb's support, there are 100 gardens in Manhattan, 175 in the Bronx, 225 in Brooklyn, and 25 in Queens.

A Brooklyn gardener is busy bundling up produce for shut-ins and senior citizens. In the Bronx thirty to forty gardeners raise enough fruit and vegetables to supply the neighborhood throughout summer and fall.

As Malinda locks up at the end of each day she can feel satisfied because the garden has once more nourished and made people happy. "This process of giving life and defeating the obstacles given to us in the city is just plain energizing."

"*Odd as I am sure it will appear to some, I can think of no better form of personal involvement in the cure of the environment than that of gardening. A person who is growing a garden, if he is growing it organically, is improving a piece of the world.*" — WENDELL BERRY

"We are guests in the animals' parks and should leave nothing but footprints behind. An ecosystem is very frail. If even the simplest organism is disrupted, the effects are phenomenal."

— LYNN ROGERS

As dawn breaks in the Minnesota wilderness, the night sounds of howling wolves and calling loons give way to the chatter of sparrows interspersed with the occasional screech of a bald eagle.

In this virgin land, black bears lumber across the moss-laden forest floor, sniffing for food and sharing the habitat with white-tailed deer that nibble nonchalantly on leaves and berries. All is as it has been for hundreds of years—except for an intruder who approaches from the edge of a clearing. Wildlife biologist Lynn Rogers has arrived for work. The forest is his office and the ways of the animals are what he studies. Lynn has devoted his life to animal research—the last twenty-two years to the black bear alone.

"I love the wilderness," Lynn says, walking confidently through brush and marsh. "You can see a whole life cycle right in front of you." All around are signs of life and death: fallen trees lie on the forest floor surrounded by flourishing aspens, paper birches, and white pines.

He bends down to pick a sprig of bright blue berries and pops a few into his mouth. "A vital forest is a functioning ecosystem, and my work is about preserving plant and animal life." Lynn wants people to understand that with every species lost in the chain of life, we humans are much closer to extinction. Every link lost weakens the entire chain, bringing it closer to collapse.

Focusing on bears happened quite by accident for Lynn. "I landed a summer job back in nineteen sixty-seven trapping black bears. I was so excited to be working with such an interesting animal that I hustled from morning till night. Up until that summer, the most bears anyone had caught in Michigan was twenty-eight. I caught that many in just one month."

These days Lynn Rogers spends most of his time feeding a computer with data that will then be passed on to the U.S. Forest Service. Near where he sits in his office hangs a plaque with a saying that could in fact be Lynn's creed:

LET MAN DECIDE UPON HIS FAVORITE ANIMAL,
LEARNING ITS INNOCENT WAYS. LET HIM LEARN TO
UNDERSTAND ITS SOUNDS AND MOTIONS—THE ANIMALS
WANT TO COMMUNICATE WITH MAN.

There is no question in Lynn Rogers's mind that he chose an intelligent and valuable animal. "Since the black bear lives closer to the land, but in a similar fashion to man and in much the same habitat, its population and health can tell us about the quality of the land upon which we, too, depend." And by working to preserve and protect the bears' habitat, he is keeping intact the homes of other species of wildlife, as well as preserving the wilderness areas and their virtues for people.

"I view the biggest problem I'm dealing with as just plain loss of habitat." By studying the bear and its forest habitat, Lynn and his team are hoping to save hundreds of plants and animals that we may currently know nothing about. "I'm always anxious to get humans interested in anything wild," he says with a wry smile.

eat, how much territory a mother claims for her cubs, what trees they use to escape into.

"We radio-collared one hundred and six bears and when the females gave birth we tagged their cubs. Eventually, when they were old enough, we radio-collared the cubs. Now we have researched the habitats of three to four generations of bears."

In order to collect data on these radio-collared bears as well as closely following three particular bears, Lynn has help from volunteers sent by Earthwatch, an environmental organization.

A lifetime of researching animals in the wilderness has required Lynn to follow the bears by air, on foot, by van, and by snowmobile. He has seen where animals have resided for hundreds of years, immune from the crush of civilization.

"In the beginning I just did air spots," Lynn says, referring to the hundreds of hours he flew in an airplane. "We'd watch for hours as they traveled, fed, fought, and mated."

After several years Lynn became more curious and wanted to get closer. He began trapping bears, fitting them with radio collars, releasing them, and going into the woods on foot or by snowmobile to watch how they lived. He recorded everything he saw: how often bears eat, what they

Lynn carefully checks sedated bear after removal from barrel trap.

Occasionally Lynn accompanies the volunteers when they do their fieldwork, recording information and putting radio collars on trapped bears. "I need to get into a forest a few times a week," he says, "or I'd go crazy!"

As the team approaches a barrel trap, they walk carefully so as not to frighten the animal inside. Lynn sedates the bear, then opens the door and cautiously pulls the animal out. "Look what we have here," he gushes, holding up a cuddly black yearling that looks like a giant teddy bear. "Nice bear," Lynn continues, patting the frightened animal.

Before taking her pulse, blood samples, and weight, he urges the group to get up close. "Look into her eyes. You'll see what an intelligent animal she is."

Lynn's enthusiasm for bears is apparent to everyone who meets him. He explains that bears have no natural enemies (except man, perhaps), and that in former times bears were master of their domain. They have a strong sense about the

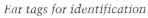
Ear tags for identification

cycles of nature and therefore are very helpful to anyone studying the connection between animal behavior and ecology.

His last task with the yearling is to attach tags to her ears. Since she will grow a lot in the next year, he must wait a little longer before he fits her with a radio collar.

The following day Lynn's manner is less jovial, more businesslike. He is searching for one particular bear—a three-year-old female named Gerry that he has been tracking for three years. Gerry has become a nuisance in nearby camps, and Lynn must divert her before someone tries to shoot her.

With a motorcade of Earthwatchers in attendance, Lynn drives up and down the back roads hoping to pick up a signal from Gerry's radio collar. During this daylong hunt, Lynn talks a lot about the bears he knows so well.

"Unfortunately, people see bears as ferocious," he says. "Nothing could be farther from the truth. People in the wilderness are more likely to die of a snakebite or a bee sting than a bear attack, but the media always reports on the bear. I'm out to prove that bears are man's friend, not his enemy. They're really unconcerned with people. While they might kill other animals, they truly prefer feasting on berries and vegetation."

Suddenly there is a beep from the radar equipment. Lynn slams on the brakes, then leaps from his vehicle, radar in hand, and follows the sound into the bush.

Walking carefully, like a bear, Lynn tunes in his senses, looking for clues that might show him a bear is nearby.

About a quarter of a mile into the thicket he halts. "Scat," he whispers, bending down to inspect fresh bear droppings. "She's nearby." He scans the area and smiles when he spots brush that has recently been flattened. Tiptoeing, he makes his way deeper into the woods and finds what he's looking for: the 210-pound Gerry is crouched under a huge bush. Her warm, chocolate eyes gaze apologetically at a very relieved Lynn Rogers.

"C'mon, Gerry," he says, coaxing her with some sunflower seeds. "We've got to get you away from here."

Without further persuasion, Gerry rises and ambles out toward the edge of the woods.

Lynn opens his van door and the bear climbs in. Bear and man head back to the laboratory.

Rejected by her mother when she was just three months old, Gerry needed a nursing mother to adopt her. Lynn was called upon to help. "She was sent to us from Michigan," he recalls. "I went to the airport to pick up this little four-pound ball of fur and found everyone standing around gawking. I immediately got down on my hands and knees, and as the cub approached, we touched noses. I let her smell my breath—that's how bears get to know one another. The little cub went nuts! She liked me."

Knowing that the third month of a bear's life is when social ties are developed, Lynn needed to get Gerry off to a mother bear as soon as possible. He didn't want her to prefer people to bears. He found a mother willing to accept her. But the little cub never forgot the fact that people are okay, too.

"She's a wild bear who likes people," Lynn says. "That's why I'm worried about releasing her just anywhere."

Although most people in the area have heard of the "bear man" and might recognize the bright yellow radio collar, there's always the chance that she will wander into the wrong yard and be shot.

Back at the lab he consults his maps along with other members of his team. "I've got to think like a bear," he reminds himself. "Now what will be Gerry's main concern in a new place?" He answers his own question: survival. He must find a spot with some appropriate vegetation, few houses, and a stand of white pines, which she can use as refuge from danger.

"I did this a bit unprepared," he murmurs. "This being the second time in a week people have complained about Gerry, I went running." It was only a few years ago that one of Lynn's study animals was shot and killed by a hunter. Lynn fought for and secured a twenty-seven-mile protected area so that the bears would be safe. "For whatever reason, Gerry keeps wandering off," he continues. "I hate to do it, but I'm afraid I'll have to release her outside the safety zone."

One hour later, some twenty-five miles southeast of his lab, Lynn Rogers opens the van door and sends Gerry off into unknown territory.

Her thick brown coat glistens in the sun as she sways up a hillside, carrying her bulky body with grace and strength. Lynn waits a few minutes and then, unable to resist the research possibilities that might come from his transplanted bear, darts up the hill and follows her to her resting place.

"Isn't it amazing how something so big can travel so quietly?" Lynn whispers. "I feel quite privileged to be on the inside of this bear's life."

Because they developed an unusually friendly relationship from the beginning, Gerry never considered Lynn a threat, as other bears might. "When we follow some of the others, they are scared and let us know it," Lynn says. "We must keep a respectable distance. But not Gerry."

In time Gerry sits down and ever so gradually stretches out until she finds a restful position. Mosquitoes buzz about her head and chipmunks scamper over and under her hind legs.

Taking a place beside her on the forest floor, Lynn talks quietly, soothing the overexcited animal. Chief Seattle once said, "If all the beasts were gone, man would die from great loneliness of spirit." It's apparent from witnessing Lynn's relationship with bears that Chief Seattle was right.

"It's true," Lynn admits. "Nobody would feel more lonely than me if the animals were to disappear."

Lynn checks the artery in Gerry's leg to take her pulse.

Gerry reaches for Lynn, touching his hand with her paw. "She's feeling secure now," he whispers. "This bear is unique in that she is a wild bear who allows touching. From her we can learn things we can't get from other bears."

Lynn wraps his arm around a nearby tree to brace himself in a position necessary to monitor changes in heart rate that will add to his growing information about prehibernation behavior.

A studied look transforms this man into a serious researcher. The bear, meanwhile, settles into deep sleep, although one ear is cocked, the flap flipped back tight on the scalp, ready to react to foreign noises.

As she falls into an even deeper sleep, Gerry rests her head against Lynn's neck and moves her paw across his chest.

This relationship between man and animal occurred because of one man's quest to understand how we are all interrelated. Bears and other wildlife are part of the world, and we humans are animals alongside them. Who's to say one is more significant than the other?

For Lynn Rogers this has been another full day. He truly believes that all living things are equal and that humans shouldn't think they have the right to abuse the wilderness. Lynn feels strongly about supporting species that have existed for millions of years. Allowing just one species and its environment to vanish may mean losing forever the cure to a disease or the solution to a famine.

His research on bears will, he hopes, influence authorities to work toward the preservation of wilderness and all creatures that inhabit it.

"If we pollute the world to the extent that animals can't live," Rogers warns, "there will be ramifications for us humans. We're doing all this work for the web of life. It is our hope that everyone who lives on this earth will realize the interconnection before it's too late."

"If a war of races should occur between the wild beasts and Lord Man, I would be tempted to sympathize with the bears." —JOHN MUIR

Afterword

When we started out to do a book about people caring for the land, waters, and animals, we were delighted and encouraged by the philosophies and the devotion we found. Not only were we impressed by these individuals and the organizations that support them, but through them we also found other earth keepers. In upstate New York there is a 92-year-old woman who invented an organic soil starter so potent and rich that it can revive dead and dying soil. A *Clearwater* crew member had sailed with an international crew from the U.S.S.R. to the United States testing the ocean waters all the way for chemicals and other debris. We also climbed to the top of a Minnesota mountain to gaze upon a field of contraptions designed to collect air and water in order to check for acid rain and pollution. And while in the area, we met people protecting the wolf from extinction and others working hard to save the bald eagle. It was heartwarming to watch forest rangers canoe through the Boundary Waters teaching campers about low-impact camping, while at the same time assessing the health of the lakes and forests. And we heard of student groups who spend entire summers and semesters constructing trails in national parks and reclaiming areas after natural disasters, such as the Yellowstone fires. And others who spend their spare time patrolling hundreds of miles of our nation's rivers, testing the waters for signs of illegal dumping.

Our work on this project was both humbling and inspiring, leaving us both with a new respect for the land that we are privileged to share with other living things.

Joan says: "I no longer walk through the woods near my Cape Cod cottage without noticing a new kind of toadstool or marveling at the variety of plant life living in a pine forest. I cling to the path now, not wanting to disturb any of the species that grip the moist soil. And during the winter when I cross-country ski, I feel honored sharing the woods with deer and bear, birds, and small animals whose tracks in the snow remind me that I am a visitor in their home.

"I've also noticed that people who frequent the beach where I swim seem more conscious of the frail shoreline and leave little or none of their garbage behind at the end of the day. And they pay attention to the signs urging them to stay away from the nesting areas of sea birds and off the fragile dunes."

George says: "I cannot help but feel a profound respect for the people I have photographed for this book. They are devoting their energies to preserve and protect that which is natural and endangered on our earth. Listening to and seeing what they have to share has enriched my life and I think made me a better inhabitant of the world."

All this tells us that the news is good—there is hope for the survival of the planet and a newfound respect for all living things as long as each and every one of us takes on the important job of earth keeping.

Environmental organizations you can contact for further information on helping care for the earth.

Earth Island Institute
300 Broadway, Suite 28
San Francisco, CA 94133-4529

Operation Greenthumb
49 Chambers Street, Rm# 1020
New York, NY 10007-1209

Earthwatch
319 Arlington Street
Boston, MA 02172-3506

Sierra Club
730 Polk Street
San Francisco, CA 94109-7813

Greenpeace
1436 U Street NW
Box 3720
Washington, DC 20009-3997

Student Conservation League
Box 550
Charlestown, NH 03603-0550

INFORM
381 Park Avenue South
New York, NY 10016-8806

United States Environmental Protection Agency
401 M Street SW
Washington, DC 20024-2610

National Audubon Society
666 Pennsylvania Avenue SE
Washington, DC 20003-4319

World Wildlife Fund
1250 24th Street NW
Washington, DC 20037-1124